M000236988

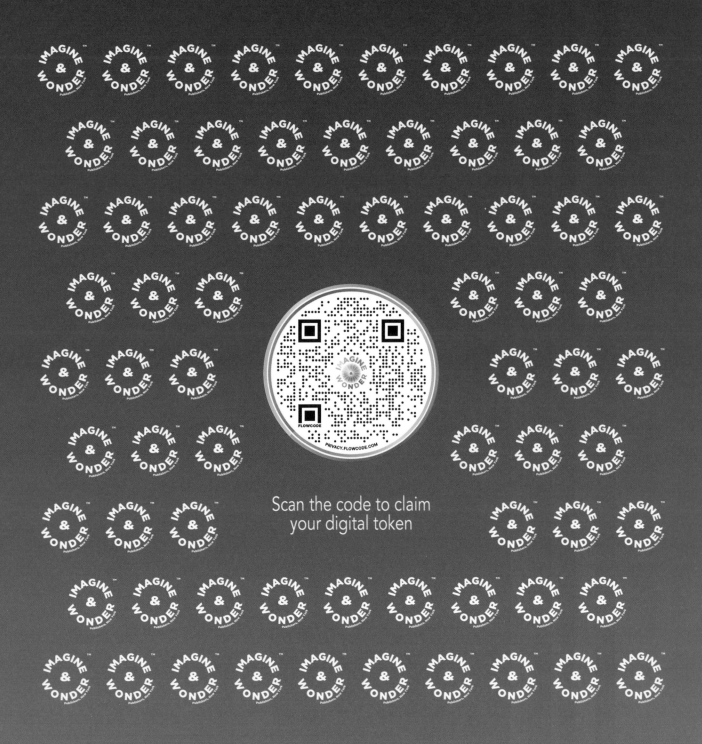

Scan the code to claim
your digital token

# WHEN WAS WE FAB

by Judith Kristen

Art by Eric Cash

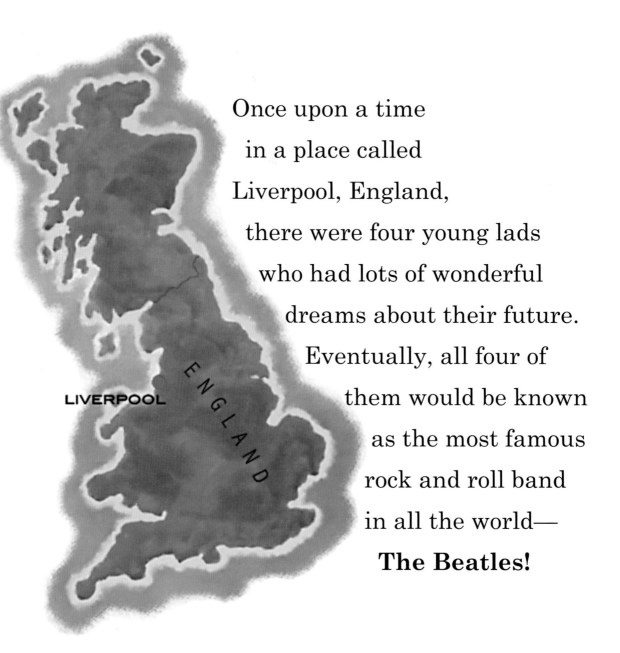

LIVERPOOL ENGLAND

Once upon a time
in a place called
Liverpool, England,
there were four young lads
who had lots of wonderful
dreams about their future.
Eventually, all four of
them would be known
as the most famous
rock and roll band
in all the world—
**The Beatles!**

It's good to dream!

One of those four
boys was named
John Lennon.
John was born
on Ocober 9th,
1940. John loved
to draw and
write stories
when he was just
a lad—and he was
very good at it!

John's father's name was Alfred. Alfred was a merchant seaman and was seldom at home with his family. John's mother's name was Julia. Julia was a woman who loved life. She even knew how to play a ukulele! Sadly, Julia died when John was just a teenager. Because of his early family situation, John went to live with his Aunt Mimi.

The lovely home that John lived in with Mimi was called Mendips.

Isn't it cool to have a house with its own name?

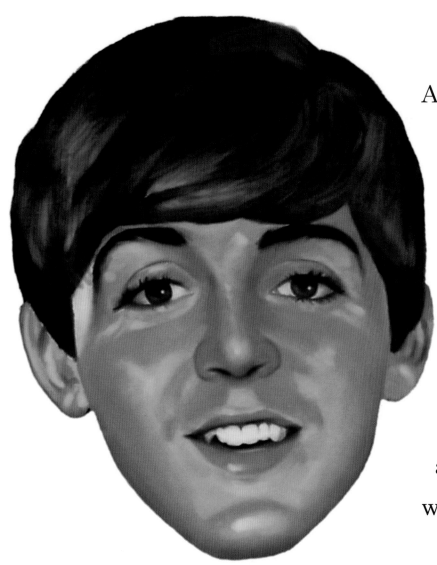

Another one of those four young lads was born on June 18th, 1942. His name was James Paul McCartney—but everyone called him Paul. He was left-handed, a lot of fun, and he was also very smart.

Paul's father's name was James. He was a hard-working cotton salesman. His Dad loved to play music and to read— so did Paul. Paul's mother, Mary, died when he wa s a young boy too. Mr. McCartney adored Paul and his younger brother, Michael very much.

Even though it was difficult at times to be a single dad, Paul and Michael grew up in a wonderfully kind and loving family.

Weren't they lucky to have such a nice dad?

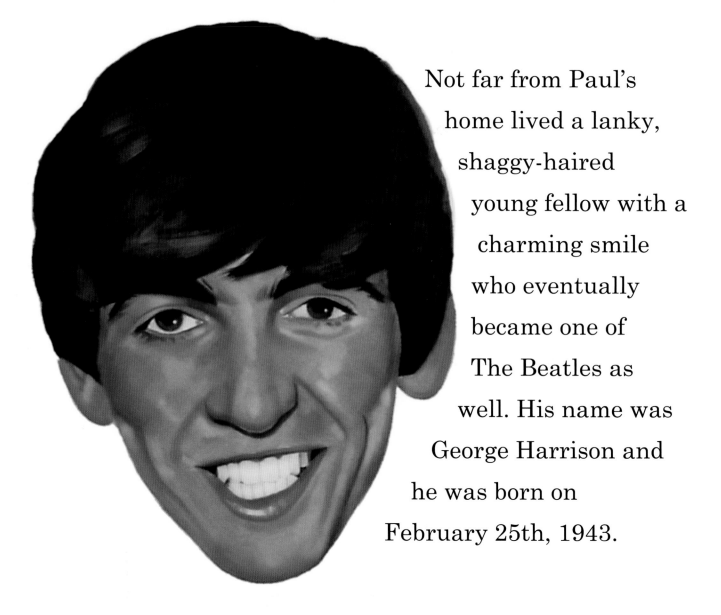

Not far from Paul's home lived a lanky, shaggy-haired young fellow with a charming smile who eventually became one of The Beatles as well. His name was George Harrison and he was born on February 25th, 1943.

George's mother's name was Louise. His father's name was Harold. George had two older brothers, Harry and Peter, and a beautiful sister, also named Louise.

They all lived in a tiny two-bedroom home but there was enough love in that house to fill a mansion.

George's mother was a very happy homemaker. George's dad was a bus driver. The big green bus he drove was the number 81.

I like to ride on a bus.

Don't you?

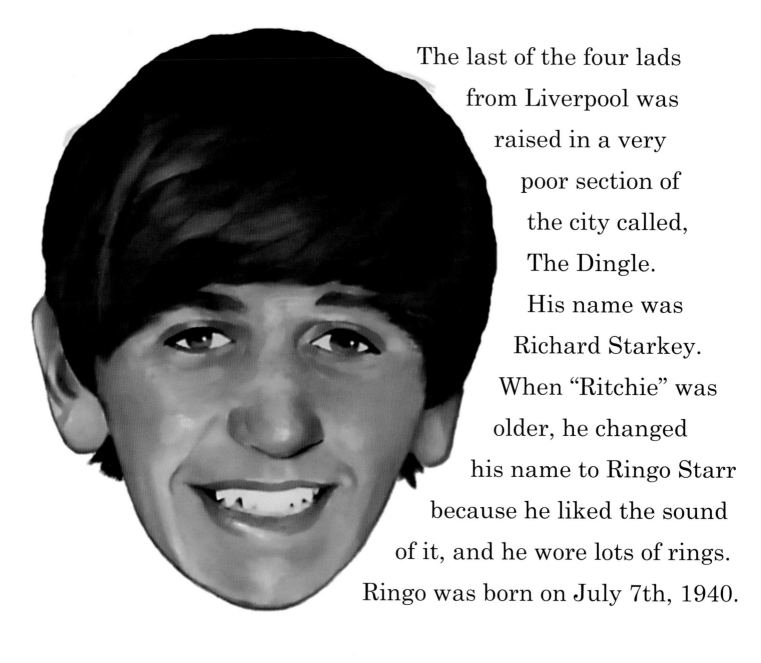

The last of the four lads from Liverpool was raised in a very poor section of the city called, The Dingle. His name was Richard Starkey. When "Ritchie" was older, he changed his name to Ringo Starr because he liked the sound of it, and he wore lots of rings. Ringo was born on July 7th, 1940.

Ringo's mother's name was Elsie. She loved her son with all her heart. Ringo was quite sickly when he was a little boy, but his family took very good care of him.

Ringo never knew much about his birth father, but he had a stepdad named Harry who loved him as if he was his own.

Even through all of his childhood hardships, Ringo kept his wonderful sense of humor and his spirited good nature.

Ringo's family was poor, but they were rich in all the ways that really mattered.

All four lads grew up and
did the things we all do
as young children and young
teenagers.
They went to school,
enjoyed the company of their friends,
went to the movies, rode bicycles,
drank lots of tea (tea is the most
popular drink in England)
and they visited the seaside
—but most of all—
they loved to listen to music!

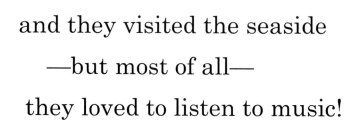

When the four of them were young teenagers the popular music in Liverpool was called Skiffle. Skiffle music was a very different kind of music.

Skiffle bands used lots of unusual instruments: washboards, tea chest basses, old drinking jugs, cigar box fiddles, comb and paper kazoos, as well as some regular instruments such as guitars and banjos.

Do you think you would like to play in a Skiffle band? I think that would be **lots** of fun!

The boys also liked to listen to the very early rock and roll records that were shipped in from America.

U.S.A.

And that's when the magic really began!

Their most favorite
musicians were:
    Elvis Presley,
    Carl Perkins,
    Buddy Holly,
    and Little Richard.

Do you like
rock and roll music?
I bet you do!

John Lennon was so inspired by rock and roll that he started his own group called, The Quarrymen. One day John's group was asked to perform at the Woolton Parish Church Garden Fete in Liverpool—and happily, they said yes!

The date was July 6th, 1957.

Paul McCartney was in the audience that day and he really liked what he heard. He enjoyed the music, but he especially liked John's style, charm, and sense of humor.

That very day, in the nearby church auditorium, a mutual friend named Ivan Vaughn introduced Paul to John.

John liked Paul straight away.

He was a good guitar player, a great singer, and a handsome lad as well!

So, of course, Paul became a band member—and John's very dear friend.

George Harrison was also a very dear friend of Paul's—and a pretty good guitar player to boot!

George auditioned to be part of the band as the three lads rode through Liverpool on a double-decker bus. George played a song called "Raunchy" on his guitar for John, and John loved it!

Then, of course, George became a band member too!

So at that time, there were three very good friends who were also three very wonderful guitar players, and fabulous singers as well. That was great, but they needed someone the play the drums!

Soon, another young boy joined the band and became their drummer. He was a very good-looking lad from Liverpool. His name was Pete Best.

Just around the same time, a school friend of John's also became a member of the group. His name was Stuart Sutcliffe. Stu was an extremely creative and talented artist—and he even played a bass guitar!

In what ways are you creative?

The band went through several names before finally settling on the one that we all know today. After The Quarrymen, they were called:

The Nurk Twins,

The Blackjacks,

Johnny and The Moondogs,

Silver Beats, The Beatals,

and The Silver Beetles.

Then, one night, as legend 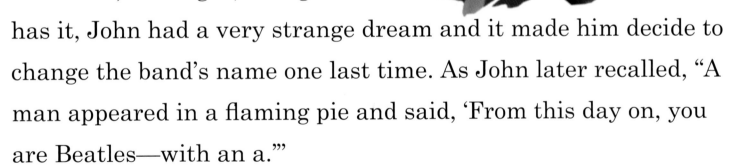 has it, John had a very strange dream and it made him decide to change the band's name one last time. As John later recalled, "A man appeared in a flaming pie and said, 'From this day on, you are Beatles—with an a.'"

So, there they were: John, Paul, George, Stuart, and Pete—now called, The Beatles!

It took The Beatles quite a few years of very hard work to become a success—even in their own hometown. They traveled all around England, and even far, far away to play in a city called Hamburg, Germany. They loved Germany, and Germany loved The Beatles! The lads played in many clubs there—sometimes for twelve hours a day, seven days a week!

They loved what they were doing, but it was still a **lot** of work—and with very little pay. There was even a time the lads felt so discouraged that they all decided to call it quits—and for a few weeks, they did! But that didn't work out very well. They were miserable without their music, without their dreams—and without each other. They knew that being part of a rock and roll band was what they were meant to do.

And lucky for all of us, the music won out. The Beatles were a band once again—and the world was about to become a much happier place.

But, as time moved on, certain things changed. Sadly, Stuart passed away in Hamburg at the age of twenty-one. As for Pete Best, John, Paul, and George felt that he was no longer right for their particular "sound" and so Pete was asked the leave the group.

Since Ringo Starr was already a well-known drummer in Liverpool, and because his personality fit the group perfectly, he was the only one they asked to become their official drummer. And in the end, as you know, that worked out just fine.

Soon, their long Hamburg days and nights were over and all that hard work began to pay off. Back in their homeland, there dreams were starting to come true!

By then, The Beatles were so popular in Liverpool they played at The Cavern Club 292 times. Now that's really popular!

In fact, The Beatles became so popular

all over Great Britain

that they were asked to appear

at a Royal Variety Performance.

The event took place on November 4th, 1963,

at the Prince of Wales Theatre in London,

in the presence of the Queen Mother

and her daughter, Princess Margaret.

Can you imagine that?

How exciting!

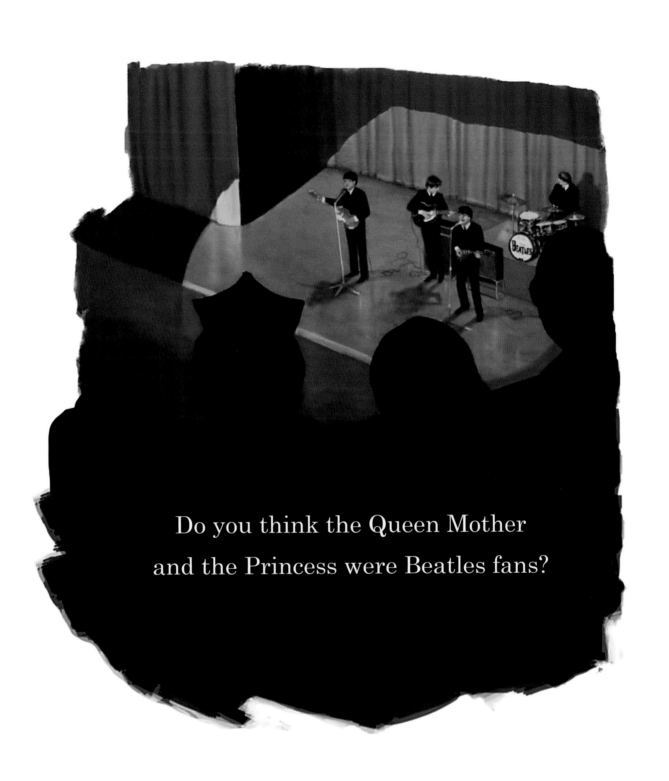

Do you think the Queen Mother
and the Princess were Beatles fans?

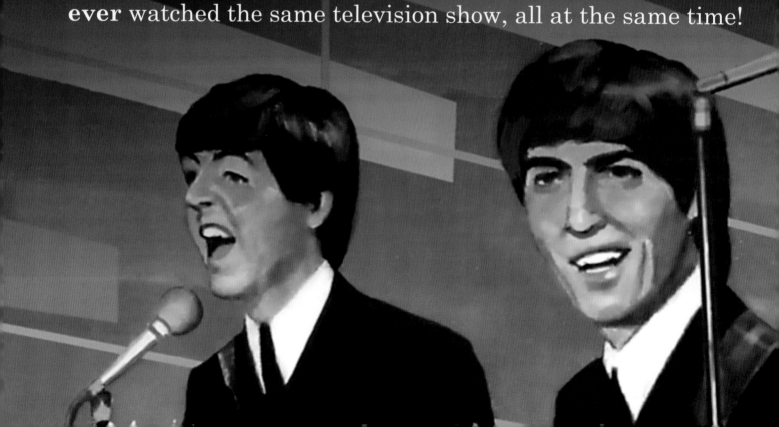

Not long after their Royal Performance, some people in America heard about The Beatles and the lads were asked to come to The United States to play their music on television. The program they played on was called, The Ed Sullivan Show. It was the most popular show in America at the time. And on February 9th, 1964, seventy-three million people tuned in to watch The Beatles perform five of their most popular songs! That was the largest number of people who **ever** watched the same television show, all at the same time!

Teenage girls **loved** The Beatles, but they were popular with teenage boys as well! In fact, lots of adults way back then liked them too! Soon, those four young lads from Liverpool were loved the world over.

Their music filled our hearts and we danced and smiled and sang along every time we heard one of their records play!

And from then on, as they say, the rest is history.

And so, here we are many, many years beyond those times when four young lads from Liverpool dreamed dreams that somehow came true for all of us.

John, Paul, George, and Ringo
**The Beatles**
Gave the musical world its
Happily Ever After.

And isn't that the best
way to end a story?
It sure is!

Scan this QR code with your phone camera for more titles **(and more Beatles)** from Imagine and Wonder

**Your guarantee of quality**
As publishers, we strive to produce every book to the highest commercial standards.
The printing and binding have been planned to ensure a sturdy, attractive publication
which should give years of enjoyment. If your copy fails to meet our high standards,
please inform us and we will gladly replace it. admin@imagineandwonder.com

© Copyright 2021 Imagine & Wonder Publishers, New York
All rights reserved. www.imagineandwonder.com
ISBN: 9781637610077 (Hardcover)
Library of Congress Control Number: 2021906474

Printed in China by Hung Hing Off-set Printing Co. Ltd.

Scan the QR code to find other
amazing adventures and more from
www.ImagineAndWonder.com